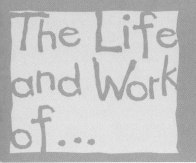

The Life and Work of...

Jackson Pollock

Leonie Bennett

Heinemann
LIBRARY

www.heinemann.co.uk/library
Visit our website to find out more information about **Heinemann Library** books.

To order:

 Phone 44 (0) 1865 888066

 Send a fax to 44 (0) 1865 314091

 Visit the Heinemann Bookshop at www.heinemann.co.uk/library to browse our catalogue and order online.

First published in Great Britain by Heinemann Library, Halley Court, Jordan Hill, Oxford OX2 8EJ, part of Harcourt Education.
Heinemann is a registered trademark of Harcourt Education Ltd.

Editorial: Nancy Dickmann and Tanvi Rai
Design: Ron Kamen and Celia Jones
Illustrations: Maureen Gray
Picture research: Mica Brancic
Production: Séverine Ribierre

Originated by Repro Multi Warna
Printed and bound by South China Printing Company, China

ISBN 0 431 09329 6
08 07 06 05
10 9 8 7 6 5 4 3 2 1

British Library Cataloguing in Publication Data
Bennett, Leonie
    The life and work of Jackson Pollock
    759.1'3
A full catalogue record for this book is available from the British Library.

Acknowledgements
The Publishers would like to thank the following for permission to reproduce photographs: Corbis/Burckhardt Rudolph/Corbis Sygma/ARS, NY and DACS, London 2004 p. **4**, **16**, **22**; Art Institute of Chicago/ARS, NY and DACS, London 2004 p. **17**; Bridgeman Art Library/Peggy Guggenheim Collection, Venice/ARS, NY and DACS, London 2004 p. **19**; Bridgeman Art Library/Private Collection/ARS, NY and DACS, London 2004 pp. **7**, **13**; Bridgeman Art Library/ National Gallery of Art, Washington DC/ARS, NY and DACS, London 2004 p. **5**; Corbis/Burckhardt Rudolph/Corbis Sygma/ARS, NY and DACS, London 2004 p. **24**; Guggenheim Museum / ARS,NY and DACS, London 2004 p. **27**; Hulton pp. **14**; **24**; Joslyn Art Museum/ARS, NY and DACS, London 2004 p. **21**; Martha Holmes/Time Life Pictures/Getty Images p. **18**; Museum of Modern Art, New York © 2003, Digital Image, The Museum of Modern Art, New York/Scala, Firenze/ARS, NY and DACS, London 2004 pp. **11**, **15**, **25**; Pollock-Krasner House and Study Center, East Hampton, NY pp. **6**, **9**, **26**; The Metropolitan Museum of Art, George A.Hearn Fund, 1957, (57.92)/ ARS, NY and DACS, London 2004 p. **23**.

Cover painting (*White Light*, 1954) reproduced with permission of Corbis/Francis G. Mayer/ARS, NY and DACS, London 2004.

Contents

Any words appearing in the text in bold, **like this**, are explained in the Glossary.

Who was Jackson Pollock?

Jackson Pollock was one of the best-known American artists of the 20th century. He lived and worked in New York in the 1940s and 1950s.

Jackson is famous for his 'drip' paintings. They are full of wild movement and crazy patterns. He made them by dripping paint on a **canvas**.

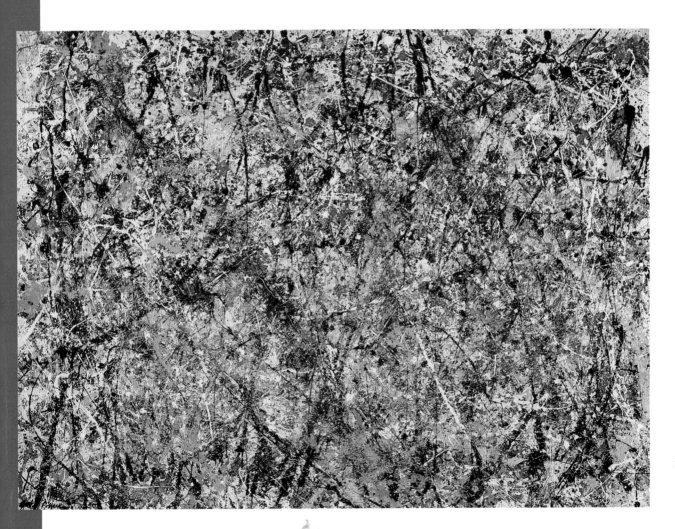

Lavender Mist: Number 1, 1950

Early years

Jackson was born on 28 January 1912 in Wyoming, USA. His family moved around the country looking for work. By the time he was ten he had lived in six homes.

When Jackson was nine his father left home to work. Jackson lived with his mother and four brothers. When Jackson was sad he drew and painted to make himself feel better.

Self portrait,
1931

School and college

Sometimes Jackson's sadness made him angry. He got into trouble at school. When he went to college to study art he was **expelled** for bad behaviour.

As a young man, Jackson **sketched** objects and people. He also copied great works of art from the past. His mother **encouraged** him. She wanted him to become an artist.

New York

When he was 18, Jackson went to New York. He worked as a cleaner and a **lumberjack** to make money, but he wanted to be a painter.

Jackson joined a group of other artists, painting **murals**. He also did his own **abstract** paintings. It was hard to recognize objects or people in them.

The Flame, 1934–38

A turning point

Jackson was very unhappy. In 1938 he was sacked from his job. At last he began to work harder on his own paintings.

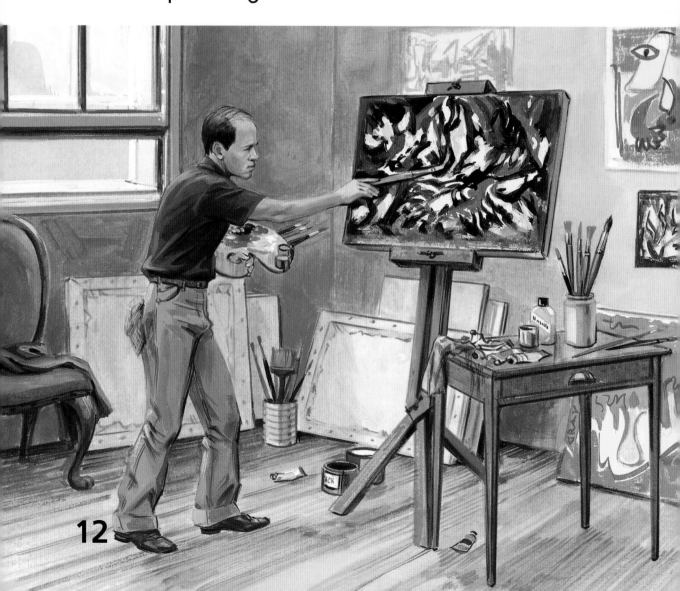

In 1941, Jackson saw an **exhibition** of **American Indian** art. He became interested in their stories and artwork. This painting shows the 'Moon-Woman' from an American Indian story.

The Moon-Woman, 1942

13

Selling his work

In 1942, Jackson met Peggy Guggenheim. Peggy had a **gallery** called 'The Art of this Century'. She showed only modern paintings and **sculptures**.

Peggy sold Jackson's work in her gallery. He had his first **solo exhibition** there in 1943. People said that this picture was the best in the show.

Stenographic Figure, 1942

Marriage

Jackson had met an artist called Lee Krasner. They got married in 1945 and went to live on a farm outside New York city.

Jackson was much happier living with Lee. She helped him to work better. Jackson did this painting in one of the upstairs bedrooms of the farmhouse.

The Key, 1946

Action painting

Jackson didn't plan his paintings or **sketch** out his ideas first. He covered the **canvas** with marks and colours without thinking.

Jackson kept moving all the time he worked.
This is called action painting. The paintings
often give us a feeling of movement.

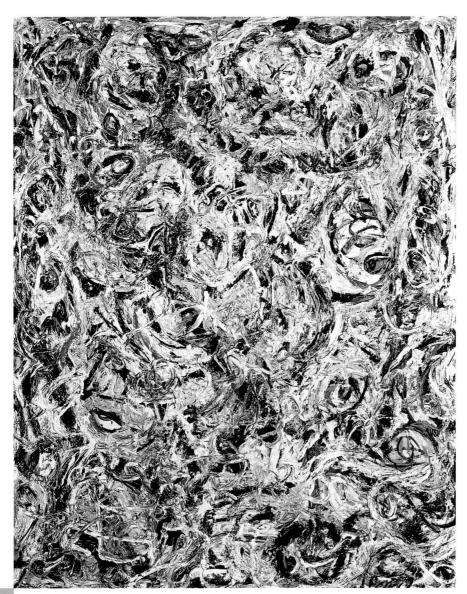

*Eyes in the
Heat*, 1946

Painting on the floor

Jackson liked the way that **American Indian** artists poured sand on the ground to make patterns. Jackson put his **canvas** on the floor. Then he poured his paint on to the canvas.

20

Jackson stopped using paintbrushes. He moved the paint about with sticks or knives. Sometimes he added sand or broken glass. This gave the paintings more **texture**.

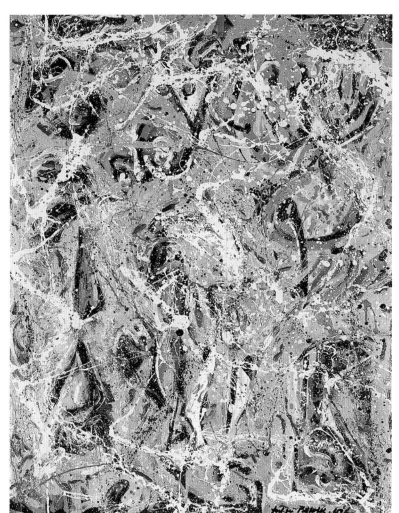

Galaxy, 1947

Drip paintings

Around 1947, Jackson started making 'drip' paintings. He worked very fast, dripping paint from a stick or brush. He walked all around the **canvas** while he worked.

The painting is a **record** of all of his movements. It is also a record of his feelings. Jackson said that modern artists painted their feelings instead of the world outside.

Autumn Rhythm (Number 30), 1950

Famous

By 1949, Jackson was famous. Some people said that he was the greatest living painter in the US. Others hated his paintings. They thought they were just a mess.

But Jackson was still not happy. He stopped giving his paintings **titles** because they were not pictures of anything. Sometimes he just gave them numbers.

One (Number 31, 1950)

A sad end

Jackson died in a car crash on 11 August 1956. He was only 44. Later that year, there was a big **exhibition** of his work in New York.

Some of Jackson's last paintings show faces and **figures**. But he had been too unhappy to paint many pictures in the last few years of his life.

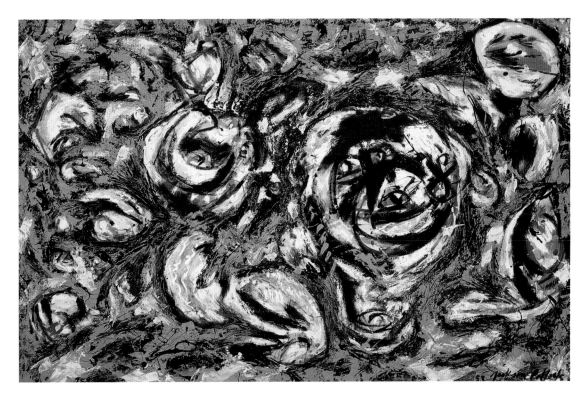

Ocean Greyness, 1953

Timeline

1912   Paul Jackson Pollock is born in Wyoming, USA on 28 January.

1913–24   The Pollocks move back and forth between Arizona and California, USA.

1921   Jackson's father, LeRoy Pollock gets a job away from home.

1928   Jackson enrols in Manual Arts training school.

1929   Jackson is **expelled** from Manual Arts for bad behaviour.

1930   Jackson moves to New York where he lives with his brother, Charles.

1930-35   Jackson works as a cleaner and a **lumberjack**. He is very poor. He paints *Self portrait*.

1934–38   Jackson painted *The Flame*.

1935   Jackson joins the Federal Arts Project – mural division.

1938   Jackson loses his job with the Federal Arts Project because he is so often absent from work.

1939   Jackson sees an **exhibition** of Picasso's work.

1941   Jackson meets Lee Krasner.

         Jackson sees an exhibition of **American Indian** art.

1942   Jackson paints *The Moon-Woman* and *Stenographic Figure*. Jackson meets Peggy Guggenheim.

1943   Jackson has his first **solo exhibition**. Peggy agrees to pay him $150 per month so that he can paint full time.

1944   Jackson sells a painting to a museum for the first time.

The She-Wolf is bought by the Museum of Modern Art, New York.

1945	Jackson and Lee marry and move into the country.
1946	Jackson paints *Eyes in the Heat* and *The Key*.
1947	Jackson begins making 'drip' paintings. He paints *Galaxy*.
1950	Hans Namuth photographs and films Jackson as he works. Jackson paints *Lavender Mist: Number 1*, *Autumn Rhythm* and *One (Number 31)*.
1953	Jackson paints *Ocean Greyness*.
1954	Jackson paints very little.
1956	Jackson has not painted in almost 18 months. He dies in a car accident on 11 August.

Glossary

abstract art that explores ideas rather than the way things look

American Indian people who lived in North America before the Europeans arrived

canvas material on which pictures are often painted

encourage give hope and confidence to somebody

exhibition show of art for the public

expelled forced to leave a school or college

figure the shape of a person

gallery room or building where art is shown

lumberjack person who chops down trees

mural picture painted on to a wall

record pattern which shows evidence

sculpture art that is not flat – often made of wood, stone or metal

sketch rough drawing

solo one person only

texture the way something feels if you touch it (eg smooth, rough, lumpy)

title the name given to something

Find out more

More books to read

Artists in their World: Jackson Pollock, Clare Oliver (Franklin Watts, 2003)

More paintings to see

Full Fathom Five, 1947, Museum of Modern Art, New York

Number 23, 1948, Tate, Liverpool

Summertime: Number 9A, 1948, Tate Modern, London

Websites to visit

http://www.jackson-pollock.com
Detailed information about Pollock's life and unique style plus a listing of where his paintings are held.

http://www.kaliweb.com/jacksonpollock/
Contains lots of links to information about Pollock's life and art.

http://www.nga.gov/feature/pollock/artist11.html
Do a search for 'Pollock' to view some of his paintings.

Index